Married to the Backslider

If My People Which Are Called By My Name Would
Humble Themselves

Married to the Backslider

If My People Which Are Called By My Name Would
Humble Themselves

Deondra Dempsey Reese

ARPress
ILLUMINATING IDEAS
EMPOWERING VOICES

ARPress
45 Dan Road Suite 15
Canton MA 02021
Hotline: 1(888) 821-0229
Fax: 1(508) 545-7580

Ordering Information:
Quantity sales. Special discounts are available on quantity purchases by corporations, associations, and others. For details, contact the publisher at the address above.

Printed in the United States of America.

ISBN-13:   Paperback   979-8-89676-367-3
                 eBook   979-8-89676-368-0

Library of Congress Control Number: 2025911908

SPECIAL THANKS

I have so many people I want to thank, but most of all I want to thank my Father in heaven. He is the reason for the inspirations in this book. I thank Jesus for His love and compassion He has bestowed upon me. I thank my family (natural and spiritual), my friends, and loved ones. **I also want to especially thank my enemies. You pushed me to be better, and God used you as a ladder to take me higher so thank you!!!**

To Sis Anne Grant. Thank you. You gave me courage and confidence to write this book. You helped me to realize that there is greatness inside of me that I should not be shamed of nor hide.

This book is dedicated to you. I hope that you will receive what it is that God has in store for you to receive in this book. I give all glory and honor to God, for it is Him who inspired me and gave such wisdom and understanding to write this book. Enjoy, I sure did.

PROLOGUE

Dear Deondra,

There is so much that I have in store for you. I want you to realize that I just can not give you all that is in store. You are going to have to go through some things and fight for what is yours. When you have to fight for what belongs to you the appreciation is greater and you understand the value. I want you to always remember that I am with you through all of the storms that are coming your way. Don't give up. You can make it. All of the hurt, pain, sorrow, agony, joy, peace, and happiness that you face needs to be written in a book. You are to be a forerunner to nations. The things you are about to go through are going to be testimonies to people you have never seen or knew existed, but I know them. The day you surrendered to me your life was not your own anymore. It's all about being about your Father's business now. Your name Deondra means Divine. The revelations that are given are divine and from above. These words are to touch the lives of many. Get to work!!!!

Your heavenly Father

THE PRAYER OF DEONDRA

I must be about my Father's business,
Lord teach me how,

Teach me to be real in what I do and say,

Teach me how to wait and how to pray,

Teach me to stay humble in the work
you have for me to do,

Keep me in perfect peace
with my mind stayed on you,

Teach me how to keep my mouth shut and my eyes
open because you said to watch and pray,

Lord keep me on my knees everyday,

Lord in my heart, mind,
and body is where I want to keep you,

Fill me with your love, joy,
and peace when a storm comes through.

Lord there are people in this world
that don't even know me

but those people are depending on you to use me to
bring them to thee,

Teach me to diligently seek you
so that I can be prepared for tests,

Because Satan is getting wise, but God you are
wisest,

Come into my heart and search it completely,

I want everything that is not of you out of me,

Lord I need you in my life I can't make it without
you,

I can't even wake up in the morning
if you don't tell me to,

Lord I want you to know I love and
honor you for just being you,

I want to thank you for my life, health,
and strength too,

Order my steps and keep me in your will,
When you are fighting my battles help me to be still,

Let my light shine so that the world can see that I
got Jesus inside of me.

QUESTION: WHO AM I?

"God, I have been so confused. I thought I knew who you wanted me to be in you. I thought I had it all figured out. I had my plans together and steps to take in order to fulfill those plans. When I began to implement the plans, I realized they were all wrong, and I was out of place. I remember the visions you gave me at age 19 and the dreams I had after the visions. What happened? Why am I not going forth?"

It's a hard thing to not know who you are. You are important to God and you need to recognize who you are in Him. I am at a point right now where I am trying to figure out who I really am. As you go along this journey with me, I want you to ask God these same questions in order to know who you are as well.

What is it about you that you want God to reveal to you?

_____

_____

_____

_____

_____

_____

_____

_____

_____

_____

_____

_____

_____

_____

ANSWER: "SURRENDER"

"If my people, which are called by my name, shall humble themselves, and pray, and seek my face, and turn from their wicked ways; then will I hear from heaven, and forgive their sin, and will heal their land." 2 Chronicles 7:4.

All I can hear God saying to me right now in that still quiet voice is to surrender. Just give up. He said stop trying to hold on to people and things and give up my will. I am kicking against the prick. What God has for me to do will and shall be done, but He is waiting on me to realize I have no choice in the matter.

It is time to seek God's face. There is such an urgency to get to know God for who He really is. Seek Him while He may be found. Do not even question what it is that God wants you to do, just do it. Say yes. Saying yes lets God know that you trust Him and that you are willing to walk by faith. Stop trying to figure God out. His thoughts are far from yours, and His ways are not like your ways. Trust and believe that He knows what is best for you. God has so much in store for you, but He is waiting on you to come back to Him. You left your first love— Jesus. You allowed the cares of this world to separate you from His Son. God is waiting for you to cry out from the depths of your soul, "I surrender, Lord, not my will but Your will be done".

I was praying to Jesus the other night because my body was going through a spiritual and physical battle. Let me explain to you what I have been dealing with. Since I was 15 years old I have been involved in relationships in a sexual manner. I got saved at 19 and realized I could not have sex anymore, so I went cold turkey. Even though I was saved and had stopped having sex, I did not realize that the sinful nature was still in me. I went through a season of loneliness. This is a season where you feel alone, depressed, heavy, and you think that you need a man in your life. So, that old me rose up and instead of letting Jesus fill that void in my life, I turned to guys. I began to date and all of those old feelings started to rise up in me. I felt the need to act on those feelings, but I could not anymore because I was saved. What is a girl to do? I told the guy that we needed to get married and we did. In return, I was able to fulfill my fleshly desires; I "got a fix".

One thing I realized about a fix is that it only lasts for a while, and then you will start looking for another one. The thing is that first high is the best high and you never experience that with a man. Jesus was my first high, and I was looking to feel that again through a man and could not. A year and a half later, I got a divorce. Now it has been over a year and I have been without a man, and that season of loneliness rose up again. This was what the physical and spiritual battle I was facing was about. My body was going through withdrawal symptoms all night. I cried unto God and asked Him if I could just call somebody to give me a fix. I knew that I could not do that, but I asked anyway because the tension was so great in me. So, I laid down, and I was about to go to sleep. The last words that came out of my mouth were, "God, you need to send me a man because I can not handle this. I am frustrated and I need to relieve this tension I can't handle being alone." I said this with anger and frustration because it was hard fighting those desires all night.

God replied to me by saying, "Life brings about change and many obstacles. There can even be a time in your life where it seems like every time you take a step forward something knocks you back 3 steps. It seems like you are getting nowhere. Imagine riding down a dirt rode during a time that it was raining. When riding down this road, you see many puddles and some of the puddles are easy to ride through or go around. Somewhere during the drive you run into a puddle that is too deep and your car gets stuck in the mud. No matter how hard you push on the gas peddle to drive your way out of the puddle you don't move. As a matter of fact, the more you push the gas peddle the worse the condition is because the tire gets deeper into the puddle. Now you have some options:

You can wait until it stops raining and the mud dries up, but that may take too long, or you can be still and wait until help comes. Sometimes when we get stuck in the mud it is a sign that we need to be still. First of all, you did not have any business going down a dirt road full of puddles, but since you did you have to wait on help. Life is very similar to this situation. When rain (weakness and temptation) comes in your life it causes your walk with me (God) to become a little wet. Rain is going to come regardless of being on a dirt road or a paved road. The paved road is righteousness. Sometimes in your righteous walk you remember old paths or shortcuts you used to take to get to destinations, so you decide that there has to be a better route and you turn to a dirt road or an old path of unrighteousness that can lead you to many puddles that you could have avoided. When you get on the wrong road you try to solve the problems yourself instead of waiting on help to come. What you must realize is that you need help when you are stuck in a puddle. You can not lift the car up and press on the accelerator at the same time. You need one person for each job. The same goes for life. You can get yourself so deep in mud sometimes that you can not even see your way out. You need someone to look down the hole that you are in and stretch out their hand to help you get out. Don't be ashamed to ask for help. There is nothing wrong with seeking help.

God knows exactly how I feel because He hit it on the nail. I feel like I am in a deep hole and I can not get out. Having an addiction to something that can be a good thing when you are married and a bad thing when you are not is hard, especially when you are not married.

I woke up the next day and went to God with the same problem as if He had not even given me an answer that night, and I heard a voice say, "I sent you a man and His name is Jesus." Then I heard Jesus ask, "Will you marry me?" I was so at ease and shocked when I heard this because I felt the realness of Jesus when He asked me. Then I asked Jesus what He meant by will I marry Him. He said, "Commit yourself unto me; become one with me; come into unity with me; get addicted to me. I promise to love you and satisfy you in ways that no man can. Just open your heart and let me in so that I can prove to you that I am all you need. I will be back for an answer soon." I began to really think about what Jesus asked me. There is a high cost to saying yes to Jesus. In the end, you better believe it is all worth it. Our problem is that we do not think about the end, we look at how things are right now. We must walk by faith and not by sight.

I sat down and began to ask myself some questions. Am I ready to forsake all men that are going to approach me and follow Jesus? Am I ready to commit myself unto Jesus? Can I live without a man in my life? Before I could even answer my own questions, guess who called me out of the blue? My ex-husband. See Satan had to make one last attempt and God allowed Him to because I believe that God knew I would stand the test this time. Isn't it like the devil to try to come in and mess up a good thing? Jesus is my good thing, and Satan tried to come in and offer me trash that I threw away over a year ago. You know trash that is old is rotten and stinks, so what can I do with it? It is strange how my ex-husband would call me in the mist of Jesus and I having a conversation about marriage. I answered the phone and all I said was hello. I had not said anything to him about the conversation Jesus and I were having, and he just start talking about how he did not want me to marry anybody, and he wanted me to wait on him to get himself together so that we could remarry. He sounded so sincere in his voice to the point that he almost convinced me to give him another chance, but this time I prayed. I already knew the answer, and I wonder why I rumbled through that old nasty trash anyway thinking I would find some good. Then I realized I was stepping back into filth and I had to retreat. Sometimes you can become so lonely and desperate that you are blinded by the truth. That's why it is important to get God's opinion on everything. I told him to forget my number, and I mean it this time.

I was so mad at myself for putting Jesus on hold for my ex-husband in order to see if he was serious and had changed. Jesus knew that I was going to do that anyway, that is why he said that he would be back for an answer. Why did I even consider my ex over Jesus anyway? You know why? Saying yes is a very high cost. Sometimes it means being without a mate, being alone or without people, or giving up things you love. If we could just get it planted in our minds that Jesus is all we need, we would live such wonderful lives. Why is it so hard to trust God? There are a million answers to that question, but what we really need to be asking is why not trust God. What harm would it do to let go of all of our problems and not worry and to cast all of our cares unto someone who wants to carry our burdens. Why carry something you don't have to?

When I think about Jesus's proposal, I ask myself "am I ready?" I want to be. I believe I am. Just in case, I pray to God that He helps me to understand what I am getting myself into and to help me to commit myself. This is one marriage in which I do not want to cheat, lust, break a vow, or disrespect my husband in anyway because I know that Jesus will be faithful in what he say and do for me. He would never leave me like all of the other men did. I know that He would never break my heart like the others did either. Lord, help me to give up and say yes to you. I surrender all to you.

This is a time and season in which we need to seek God's face while He may be found. I can hear God crying out to seek Him with all you have and to get to know him for who he really is. It is time out for playing church. God said He has enough Pharisees in the church. He is looking for those who will worship Him in spirit and in truth. God told me to take time out each day to give to Him. He blesses us with 24 hours in a day. He said to give 10% of each day to Him and watch how He blesses me. I challenge you to do the same while reading this book.

Notes: Any revelations from this section

_____

_____

_____

_____

_____

_____

_____

_____

_____

_____

_____

_____

_____

_____

_____

_____

_____

_____

_____

_____

_____

_____

_____

_____

_____

_____

_____

_____

Q: Will you marry me?

Well, Jesus has come back for His answer and I am so ready to say yes. I have all of a sudden had an overwhelming feeling to surrender my all to Jesus. I listened to the song "yes" by Shekkinah Glory and that song really started to make sense to me. The song simply says yes. Everything about you has to say yes to God, your mind, body, soul, and your will has to say yes. When you really say yes you are actually telling God you give up.

"Jesus, I say yes to your proposal. I will marry you. I will commit myself unto you. I am ready to go higher in you. I want to know about you and your Father. Teach me your ways. Prove to me that you are who you say you are. I am trusting you to take care of me like a husband would. I am trusting you to teach me the Word of God and to use me. I am trusting you to fill in this huge gap in my life."

I just felt so much peace after surrendering to Jesus. Then I thought about something, Jesus I want to present to you a holy body. I want to be pure in your eyes Jesus. I have been through a lot and I just got out of a marriage not too long ago. Jesus make me over will you? I present my body to you because it is yours now, and I ask you to place me on your Fathers will (wheel) and make me over. There are some things I may have picked up in my previous marriage and previous relationships that should not be attached to me. I may still have anger in me towards men. I do not want to bring in stuff from my past into this marriage Jesus. I do not want to compare you to any man because I know that no man can treat me better than you can. I need you to wipe it off of me. Make me into the person you want me to be. Make me holy in your sight. Spin me on your precious wheel Father and present me to your Son in a way that is pleasing to you. Just start over with me. Give me a clean slate. Give me a clean heart. Purify my mind, body, and soul. Transform my mind into the mind of Christ. Do a new thing in me. Fix me where I have been broken. Lord I need your help because I can not do these things by myself. This is a holy marriage. The best thing that I like about this marriage is that in an earthly marriage death separates you from your mate. When you marry Jesus, death can not separate you from Him, it actually brings you to Jesus, you finally get to meet your Savior.

Notes:

ANSWER: I AM THAT I AM

Jesus began to share some things with me after I said yes to Him. Now I know that you are probably thinking it is crazy to say that you are married to Jesus. Well, your body belongs to God anyway. Your body does not belong to you, its on loan, now if you are married your body is your husbands or wife's. We all actually marry Jesus when we give our life to Him. The thing is we do not realize what we are really doing when we give our life to Christ. We are committing ourselves to Him hence, entering into a marriage. I did not realize this myself until I heard Jesus ask me to marry Him. It just seemed, so real. Jesus wants to be our soul mate. He wants to be our everything. We look and search the world for friends, mothers, fathers, and even sisters and brothers because we feel that the ones we have are not worthy to be who they are or either we do not have anyone in that area of our life. We try to fill that void in our life by wasting time looking for people, when all along Jesus is waiting to fill every void in our life. God told me to stop trying to find a mother or father to replace in my life and cherish the ones I have. Then He said that until I allow Jesus to be those things I need in my life, He will not send them to me. For example, I desire to have friends. God said to allow Jesus to be my friend first then He will send true friends in my path. Another one of my weaknesses is men. God knows that if He sends a man in my path right now I will lose focus. I won't pray like I should. My focus would be on the man in my life. Jesus is trying to redirect this weakness I have for men and turn it into a strength, so that

He makes me weak. Jesus want to make me weak in the knees and bedazzled in His presence. Once Jesus can see that I will be faithful to Him with or without a man I believe He will consider sending me a husband. That is if I still desire one because once I realize who I am in this marriage and Jesus begins to spoil me, I don't know if I would want to end such a good thing. I am just going to stay in this marriage and stay committed to Jesus. I am not going to worry about anything else.

Soon after I finished saying this I heard Jesus speak to me. He said that He is my husband, friend, mother, sister, and companion. Because of Jesus, I am able to be healed, saved, set free from bondage, and delivered. If Jesus is able to be and do all of these things for me, just imagine what His Father can do. Jesus said in John 14:28, "...My Father is greater than I". I am now a part of the royal family. Jesus is my husband and God is my Father now, so whatever I need I just ask Jesus, and Jesus goes to Our Father. Since I am a part of the family, I should represent the family. It is time out for me looking broke, busted and disgusted. I should look like a queen because I am royalty now. I should lack nothing good. The earth is the Lord's and the fullness there of, so why should I lack? Why should I walk around looking like a throw away child when my Father owns the world and all that dwells therein? I also understand that when I am going through or sick, all I have to do is call on the name of Jesus. Jesus is sitting on the right hand of the Father watching me and when I call on His name that lets Him know that I acknowledge

Him. So when I get into trouble, I can hear Jesus saying to God "Father, Deondra has been calling on my name for a while now, and I see that she is in trouble, her body is sick and I need you to send healing virtue through her body. Also Father, open a door for her a job because I know that she will put me first before her job. I trust her Father."

God is so awesome. What one word in this human vocabulary can describe Him? Wonderful? Well that is good, but He is also Amazing. What about Healer? That is good as well, but He is also Provider. I do not think there is one word that can sum up who God is. That is why He called Himself "I Am". There is no word to put after am because He is who He is and that all you can say. Who would not serve a God who is that mighty and powerful that there is no one name to sum up who He is.

Q : ARE YOU READY TO FLY?

I had a dream about three weeks ago and it was very short, sort of like a vision. I just remember my grandmother Mudy sitting in a chair looking at me. She said to me that God is getting ready to take His people higher. Then I woke up. I was then reminded of a vision God gave me a long time ago when I was 19 years old. I dreamed that I was flying. I flew into different layers of the heavens and I realized that bullets were passing me. I asked why the bullets were not hitting me because there were so many of them. Then I heard a voice say, "look down". I looked down, even though I was about 35,000 feet or higher in the air, I could see the ground on earth. I saw my pastor looking up at me and praying. God then told me that he sent this man to watch over my soul, but I would eventually leave him, but not to worry because he will always be praying for me. He reminded me that one day I was going to have to leave from under him to go higher. Then a friend of mine sent me a text message asking me if I was ready to fly. Now he was talking about flying in an airplane because I had told him that I was afraid to fly on a plane. God removed that fear from me that same day, so I replied to him yes. Then he told me to say out loud that I am ready to fly. I heard the voice of God ask me the same question, and God was talking about flying spiritually or allowing Him to take me higher. So, I answered both my friend and God and said I am ready to fly. I felt so good when I said it because I am ready to go higher in God. I want my wings!

Notes:

ANSWER: LAY ASIDE EVERY WEIGHT THAT SO EASILY BESETS YOU.

After telling God that I am ready to fly and I want my wings, He told me that I have too much baggage on me to fly. I got to lay aside or take off this excess weight that I am carrying. God then began to reveal to me the things that I am carrying that are causing me to not fly. This very moment, God is giving me an opportunity to let everything out that is bothering me and lay it at His feet. I do not even know where to start.

As I sit here and look at this 1000 piece puzzle, I see myself. I feel shattered and broken just like these puzzle pieces. It seems impossible to be able to put me back together. Well I am going to try to put myself back together, but I do not know where to began. What part of my life do I want to start with. I think my heart needs to be worked on first. It is the most difficult part of the puzzle to work on. You know why? About five years ago, I let go of a five year relationship. This piece of puzzle broke my heart and I thought I would never find love again. Then I thought I found the right piece of puzzle, my ex-husband, and he broke my heart to pieces. Right now I do not trust men and I do not feel like I will ever find true love. I am almost afraid to date again because men are like kryptonite to me. They make me weak. I believe that I love too hard and that is why I get hurt. I allow them to fill my head with wishful thinking, sorry dreams, and a false inclination of what a real man is. Anyway, as I look at the puzzle, I realize that a lot of the pieces do not belong to my puzzle. They are not a part of my life or destiny. I wish I would have known this earlier.

This puzzle piece of abuse does not belong. These pieces of low self-esteem, depression, and sickness do not belong either. Oh, lets not forget this piece of lying and cheating. How did these pieces get into my box? Who put them there? Was it me? What do I do with them? These pieces are slowing down my destiny. These pieces are causing me to not be able to see my visions clearly. These pieces have caused me to be bitter and have taken away my praise and joy. I must get rid of them immediately. Well, Father, I must be honest and say that I also have an issue with trusting your people. It is not that I do not believe in you or the power you can present through your people. It is the simple fact that some of your people abuse the power you give them and in return, people like me have to suffer and get hurt.

I went through a storm where I was dealing with a woman who claimed to be a prophet of God. This lady was awesome to me. She taught me not to be ashamed of praising you (God) in public because she was very charismatic. Well, we became very good friends and many people loved her. One day I began to get sick, and that one day ended up being eight weeks. For eight weeks I was vomiting from 7:30am- 5pm everyday. I could not hold any food down. Every time I thought about the name Jesus or praying I got sick to my stomach. These were the prayers that she prayed against me. I was suicidal, depressed, oppressed, and stressed. I did not know what was happening to me. I finally realized that it was witchcraft, but I did not know who was doing this to me. God later revealed to me that it was this "prophet" in whom I put a lot of trust in. The "prophet" of God as she would call herself. God told and showed me that this lady was poisoning my body with deadly poison everyday and this caused me to vomit daily. God said her assignment was from Satan himself to destroy me, but the Spirit of God lifted up a standard against her and would not let it be so.

Because of this abuse I received, I have trouble trusting people in the church. I saw this lady in the spirit and she looked like a witch beyond witches that I can not explain. How is it that you can allow these type of people in your house to destroy your people Father? Then, after I got out of that storm, I had to deal with a pastor who was married being infatuated with me. This pastor was well known and liked in the community and I did not know what to do or who to talk to, so I just put him in your hands. Later, I dealt with this other woman who claimed to be a prophet, but she was trying to suck all of the anointing out of me. I call these people leaches, they have no source of power, so in order to survive they have to live off of someone with power. Then I dealt with people from other churches trying to get me to join their church and help them (more leaches). I just could not take all of that. So know that it is time for me to fly, I have become a little afraid because I began to look at the war wounds from the church. Most of my battles have been within the church, I do not mean my church but rather the body of Christ. That is why I said it is hard for me to trust your people. It is hard to find many to trust. This is the very reason why so many people are non believers.

We, the body of Christ are not living what we preach. We are talking the talk but not walking the walk, and therefore confusing the world and making people like me look bad because the world thinks that we are all alike. We need to get it together. Father help us.

Another thing that is bothering me is my previous marriage. I was hurt deeply by my ex-husband. I put my heart in his hands and he returned it to me all broken to pieces. When I see him now I get angry because I can not believe that he treated me so badly. I took a lot of stuff badly. I took a lot of stuff from him that I did not have to take in order to save our marriage, and he still ended up hurting me. I literally begged him to not leave me. I gave him my whole heart and I treated him like a king, but he just would not love me. I just do not understand why. What did I do wrong to make him not want to commit to me? I know I did not do anything but it seems as if I could blame myself that at least I would have an answer.

Also, I have been without a job for a while now. I feel very low at times because I do not have money. I am tired of borrowing. I am tired of people looking at me with pity because I am always struggling. I am tired of hustling, not with drugs, but finding little gigs and ways to make money that do not last long. I want a steady good paying job where I enjoy what I do. I want to be independent and not having to depend on people to help me all of the time. I want to look like I belong to the most high God. I want to look like the daughter of a king.

Father, if you could just help me in these areas of my life I could fly high in the sky. Help me to release the hurt, anger, and shame in my heart towards my ex husband. Open up a door for me for a job where you want me to be and I am making good money. Place true men and women of God in my path that have a desire to live for you and be about your business. Lord, please remove all of this heavy weight from me because it is hindering me from flying to my highest potential. I can talk to friends about all that I have shared with you, but they do not know the whole story like you. They were not there to see me those nights I cried myself to sleep and the nights I could not sleep. They did not see me at my lowest point in my life when I wanted to commit suicide. They were not there when I felt like a nobody and could not even look at myself in the mirror. You have seen all and know all about me. They can not feel my pain they way your Son can. Hear my cry Father through your Son Jesus. I need you.

As I sat down and thought about all the things I laid before my Father, He began to speak to me. The first thing He reminded me of was when I was a freshman in college and I was somewhat a Christian, meaning I finally start believing in God because I used to be an atheist. Well, my roommate and I decided to go to church on campus that day. The preacher asked if anybody wanted to testify about the goodness of the Lord, so I raised my hand. He said to testify. I said that I was thankful that I made it through high school and into college without a father figure but through God I made it. Well after making this statement this preacher came up to me and stood in my face and start yelling at me to the point that he was spitting in my face. He yelled at me in front of about fifty students and told me not to let the devil fool me because I made a statement that was a lie. He said I did have a father figure and it was God. Then he looked at me and smirked and said "I don't care if you get mad either". Now, that old me wanted to rise up and cuss that preacher out because he was all up in my space and spitting in my face trying to make himself look good. I held my peace. I know that I said nothing wrong because I stated that I made it through God, I just stated I had no natural father figure. So after this I was extremely angry and said there is no God because God would not allow a preacher to embarrass me like that. So I turned away from God again.

About three months later I heard a voice say "everything that cries holy is not holy". I then realized that God was telling me that Satan has his crew as well trying to imitate Christians for the very purpose of deceiving God's people as he did me, insomuch that a believer turns from God.

Now I hear God making that same statement to me again that everything that cries holy is not holy. I do not have to believe every spirit but try the spirit to see if it is of God. Greater is he that is in me than he that is of this world. I have the greater power living inside of me. Then God said to me that those who are truly His do not abuse the gift that He gave them, nor do they abuse their fellow sisters and brothers in

Christ. The Lord knows those who are His. Do we? Can we decipher who is a child of God and who is not? If we can not, we need to ask for discernment because the times are going to get worse and worse where we need to know who is of God.

Second, God said to me to never put my heart in a man's hand. Man is not perfect. Man is not like God. God would never hurt us or our heart. God loves us so much that He gave His only Son for us. I hear God asking me to return the key to my heart back to Him. He will not give access of my heart to anyone that will hurt me. Then I hear God asking me what did His Son Jesus do that made me not want to commit to Him in the past? Why did I leave my first love Jesus for these no good men that cared nothing about me? What I need to do is just let everything go. If I allow Jesus to take control of my life Jesus will fill in that gap so great that I forget about my past. Lord I want to forget about my ex-husband. I want to focus on Jesus and Jesus alone. Help me Father to ease this heavy and hurting heart of mine. I give you the key, but before you lock the door to my heart, take everything out and put only your Son Jesus in. See I have a good reason why I want you to take everything out. I may have love in my heart, but it may not be the love of Christ. I may have patience or long suffering in my heart, but it may not be enough. If I have only Jesus in my heart then I know that everything in me is perfect, including perfect love which casts out all fear. There would be no room for anything or anybody else. There are pieces in my life that should not be here. Perhaps, I have pieces in my life that are missing? When you are shattered to pieces it is hard to live. It is hard to make sense of things. I was so hurt at one point in my life that I did not want to go on. I felt like just throwing in the towel. Do you know what God told me? Well actually he spoke it through someone. This person said that we all may occasionally catch hell in our lives, but when we catch it, don't hold on to it, let it go. Man, is it hard to let things go.

So, I heard God say when you find a piece of puzzle that does not belong to you, let it go. No matter how well it may appear to fit in a spot, it doesn't. It belongs to someone else. Let it go so that you can find your piece. If you ever want to know why relationships go bad in your life and why you can't find a good man, it is because you have somebody else's piece of puzzle. You have not found your piece yet. Sometimes it may take a while to find your piece but wait patiently, look diligently through the 1000's of pieces of puzzles until you find your mate. If you are wondering why you have not found a good car or home, it is because you have not found your correct piece yet. Be patient. Seek ye first the kingdom of God and he will help you find those pieces. He will give you your hearts desire, which is your correct piece of puzzle.

It is when we are broken and of a contrite spirit that God is ready to deliver. Its alright to cry. Tears are a language that God understands.

As far as a job, God said I already know what to do. If I ask I shall receive. First I have to seek ye first the kingdom of God and His righteousness and delight myself in the Lord and He will give and add these desires to me. I got to focus on my Father and He will began to open doors for me that no man can close. Thank you Father. What are your burdens that you need to let go? What are the things in your life that easily besets you or make you feel heavy when you try to fly? Give it to your Father, He is waiting for you to come to Him so that he can come to you.

Notes:

"Meet Me At the Alter, Come and Let Us Reason Together"

As I knelt down to pray, God said to meet Him at the alter. He said He has a reserved seat for me. I closed my eyes and began to pray. God showed me myself in a beautiful white dress. I was walking down this long aisle. I could not see what was ahead of me, but I just kept hearing this voice say to keep walking. He said my Son is waiting for you at the alter and He said please don't stand Him up this time. Now that hurt me. Can you imagine all the times we have stood Jesus up at the alter? He was ready to make a commitment with us and all we had to do was meet Him at the alter and we stood Him up. Well, even though this was a long aisle I kept walking because I wanted to see Jesus. The more I walked the more I could see this man looking at me and waiting on me to come to Him. It seemed like it took about an hour for me to make it to the alter, but I finally made it there.

Then, Jesus turned to me and I turned to face Jesus. He said, "look at me. Look at the prints on my head from the crown of thorns. The people used crowns to represent royalty and power, so the people took the crown of thorns and pressed it down on my head to try and humiliate me or show that I have no true power. Look at the hole in my side where they pierced me. The people wanted to make sure that I was good and dead, so they took a rod and pushed it through my side, and your name was still on my mind. I had to go through the whole process for you. Do you see the hole in each of my hands? Each time the people hit that nail I was thinking of you. I could have called a legion of angels to come and rescue me, but if I would have gotten up I would have lost you. I had to endure the pain for my Deondra. My hands are strong enough to carry your burdens. Look at the holes in my feet. I want you to see these signs because they are evident that I can take the pain. There is nothing on this earth that can bring harm to me. I have all power in my hands on heaven and earth. Every time the people hit the nail in my hands they hit every sin, circumstance, and problem. When I died all that was hit in my hand died, and I rose with all power in my hands over all the things that died with me. They nailed my hands for you. If you were the only person in this world and I had to come down just for you, I would not have hesitated because I love you that much. They spit on me, mocked me, cursed at me, and rejected me. I took all of that pain for you. Look at the whelps on my back. They beat me until they ripped skin off of me. I took all of that pain for you Deondra. So that every time you get sick you are already healed through my pain. You are special to me. I did not give my life, I laid down my life for you. Every wound on my body was for your healing physically, mentally, and spiritually. I have everything under control if you would only believe me. Come to me with all of your problems no matter how big or small and place your problems in my hands. You see the evidence that I can handle anything. Trust me. Do you trust me?"

After hearing what Jesus said, I heard my Father speak. I felt so vulnerable and humble in His presence. My Father said to me, "Look at my Son laying on the cross. Can you see all of the sin on that cross? The cross represented the sin of the world. I allowed my Son to carry all of the sin of this world on His shoulder and His back, including your sins. The same back and shoulder that they whipped Him all night long on was the same back that was strong enough to carry your sins. All of those wounds represents healing. The people made a mistake when they laid all of that healing (His wounds) on top of the sin of the world (the cross). Then the people nailed Him to the sins of this world. He had to just lay there and marinate on top of our sins to be able to feel and endure the sensation and pain that sin brings throughout the human body. That is why He is the perfect advocate for sin, He had to lay on sin and die to it so that He could have power over sin and conquer it. Do you know why I forsook my own Son? When He cried My God, My God, Why has though forsaken me, I thought about you, I love you that much that I forsook my Son for a moment so that you could live. Do you know why I allowed my Son to die for you? When I think about the creation of Adam. I put Adam to sleep and took something out of him (a rib) and created woman. There was greatness in Adam, she was so great that I had to put Him to sleep in order to bring it out of Him. Well, when I though of you I saw greatness. The greatness was not in Adam this time, but the greatness was in my only Son Jesus. I had to not only put my Son to sleep to bring out the greatness in Him, but I had to let Him die so that the greatness could be made manifest in the world. You are a part of that greatness. Jesus even said to the disciples that if we believed on Him, the works that He do we shall do also; and greater works shall we do because He goes to His Father (John 14:12). He had to die in order for these greater works to be made available to you. Can't you understand how much I love you? Do you trust me? Do you believe me?"

After hearing all of what Jesus said unto me I was overwhelmed. To envision the wounds Jesus took just for me. To see how Jesus still loves me in spite of all the wrong I have done and said towards Him out of ignorance. How many men do you know of that would lay down their life for a woman? How many men would allow people to drive nails in their hands and feet for a woman? I think about myself and the people in my life, and I may risk my life to save their life, but I don't think I am to the point where I will volunteer to lay my life down for anybody. Now, If I had children I probably would, but I don't have kids, so I can not see myself laying down my life. That is love. All I can say is I am sorry for not coming to Him sooner. Jesus, I trust you. Forgive me for doubting you. Help me to be strong.

Jesus replied to me, "I am your husband now. Forget about the past and look at today. Do right today. Love me today. Whatever you need just come to me, I am supposed to supply your every need. I am supposed to protect you. I will never leave you home alone where you are afraid to sleep at night. I will never strike you or call you a name that is beneath who you are. I will always respect you, love you, and treat you like the queen you are in my eyes. My Father made a good thing when He made you!"

After hearing Jesus say all of these things to me, I am speechless. All I can do now is take a nap and allow everything to really soak in. Jesus has love that is beyond my understanding and I am so glad His love is not the same as the love that man has. His love is powerful, it is strong enough that He raised Himself from the dead. It is strong enough to speak to a body that has been dead for three days and command it to come forth. That is powerful!

When I think about how bad they beat Jesus all night long and how he endured all of that pain for me, I feel like I am important to Him. He said every time they hit the nail in His hands he thought about me. Wow. He even said that he could have called on more than ten legions of angels to come to His rescue but He didn't, neither did He complain. This brings me to a remembrance of when I was in an abusive relationship. This guy and I used to fight all of the time. He was very controlling and called me all kinds of names. Every time he hit me I could hear God yelling to me to just say the word and He would destroy the guy. I felt so sorry and fearful for the guy's life that I would just cry Lord just have mercy on him, I can take the pain. What I realize now is that I am not Jesus, and it was not meant for me to take pain for anybody. The power was in me to get out of the relationship and God was ready to destroy him, but because I thought I was in love I would not give God the ok. (Now I am not saying that it is ok to stay in an abusive relationship, I am trying to make a point. If you are in an abusive relationship you need to get out). So then I thought about Jesus and how they beat Him, spit on Him, mocked Him, and belittled Him. I know that He was in a far more worse condition that I was. In the mist of all of that, Jesus said Father forgive them for they know not what they are doing. The thought had to have came to His mind to call on angels because He said if He wanted He could call them, but in the mist of being beaten He thought about you and I and said, "Don't destroy them prepare me a body. I can take the pain for them Father."

Notes:

_____

_____

_____

_____

_____

_____

_____

_____

_____

_____

_____

_____

_____

_____

_____

_____

_____

_____

_____

_____

_____

_____

_____

_____

Lay all of your problems in Jesus's hand. He has proven with evidence, through the print of the nail in His hands, that He can take the pain for you!!!!!

"Shine the Light of Heaven on My Heart"

As I sit and think on the goodness of my Father, He began to allow His Son into my heart. Now the strangest thing is, I have been saved since I was 19 years old, but I am just learning the true meaning of salvation through this book. We all ask Jesus to come into our heart when we receive salvation. Do we really know what we are asking when we do that? Jesus came into my heart and began to expose me. He is light, so He came into a place that had a lot of dark spots in it and He showed me myself. He showed me those hidden faults inside of me that I needed to get rid of. When Jesus comes into your heart, He is coming to clean it out or at least give you the opportunity to allow Him to clean it out. Jesus is not going to dwell in an unclean environment.

The first thing Jesus showed me that was in my heart was something that goes all the way back to when I was a child. I did not receive the type of attention growing up where I was hugged and told "I love you" or "good job." When I was old enough to go to school, I found a way to receive attention by being smart. Se teachers loved me from kindergarten to high school. I was the teacher's pet. I was very smart in school. When I received rewards on Honors Day so many people would pat me on the back and tell me how proud they were of me, and it made me feel so good. Once I got saved, I figured I could be the same way. If I show my intelligence people would like and accept me. The opposite happened. As a matter of fact, I did not have a chance to show my intelligence. From the start, I was looked upon as someone who is of very low intelligence. The one thing that made my skin crawl was for someone to insult my intelligence. I got to the point that I was trying so hard for people to see that I was not dumb that every chance I got to do something I tried to be extremely perfect. I wanted so much just to be accepted and patted on the back like I was in school.

Jesus had a little talk with me about myself and asked me who in this world died for me or risked their life for me. I said nobody but Him. He then asked me why am I trying to be a man pleaser. He said His Fathers house is not a play. Church is not a place to perform an act or try out for an audition for the people. Gods house is a place of worship. Jesus said His Father has enough Pharisees who praise Him with their lips and their hearts be far from Him. God is looking for people to worship him in spirit and in truth. This is a personal thing. Then Jesus said when I gave my life to Him, the world did not revolve around me anymore. All glory belonged to His Father. He said I will get my pat on the back from my Father when He says "Well done my good and faithful servant". Jesus said when my father looks at my heart He wants to see purity, praise, holiness, and love. He wants to see His Son Jesus when He sees the heart of His people.

Then Jesus showed me something else in my heart. He said keep other peoples name out of my mouth. Stop aiding people in gossip. Aiding is not necessarily gossip, but you know when you are in a conversation and other people talk about other people and you don't say anything but listen, or you laugh along with them. He said to separate yourself from ungodly conversations. Show a difference between holy and unholy. Let your conversation be yea or nay.

Then Jesus showed me my lustfulness in my heart. Man it is not pretty when the light is shined on you. Jesus said that I needed to be delivered from the lust of the eye. I already knew that was in my heart, but for Jesus to point it out just makes me feel bad.

There was a lot more of what Jesus showed me about myself. The main thing He said was to clean up my heart. So I began to search the scriptures and I went to Psalms 19:12-14. I said Father cleanse me from my hidden faults. We all have those things that we need to be delivered from that nobody knows about but you and Jesus. Those are the main things we need to get rid of. I am tired of living like this. I cried out to my Father to create in me a clean heart and renew a right spirit within me. I want to be holy in my Father's sight. I want Jesus to rest in my heart. I would rather Jesus expose me in private than for Him to expose me in front of everybody.

God is trying to get His people to come back to Him in purity. He wants to make himself known to the world, but we as His children have to get ourselves together.

I went to bible study with a friend one night, and this preacher talked about the seat of anointing. He said everyone has their own seat of anointing that God places them in. As long as we are in that seat we are protected and things just flow in our lives. Trouble comes but we have peace. Due to our disobedience and not being focused, we sometimes allow the enemy to get us out of our seat. The enemy convinces us to get out of our anointing. When we get out of our seat chaos break loose in our lives. We wonder why we can't make ends meet. We wonder why we struggle so much. We wonder why we just can't get a breakthrough. It is because we are not in our seat. We are walking in disobedience. My Father began to speak to me and said "I want to put you back in your seat, will you let me?" I said "Father I desire to be put back into my seat of anointing where I used to speak things in Jesus name and it came to pass. Where I was a willing vessel walking in no fear, laying hands on the sick and they recover. Where you spoke to me daily and gave me divine revelations. I want my seat back. Forgive me for my disobedience. I want to walk right."

I heard a voice say "woman thou art loosed". Then I felt myself being placed into another atmosphere. I fell to my face and began to cry out in the spirit. I got up and I felt like I was on cloud 9. I felt my Father's presence right beside me. It was like He had to come down Himself and handle this case. He began to clean me out from all impurity in me. I felt myself being changed in an instance. Later on, when I came to, I heard God say, "Now that I have placed you back into your seat, don't get up. Stay in your seat."

"Deondra, do you love me?"

After my Father and His Son cleaned me up and put me back together, Jesus asked me did I love Him. I said yes Jesus you know I love you. Then He said again, "Deondra do you love me?" I thought for a minute. Do I really love Jesus? It seems like I am always leaving Jesus for something whether it be a man or a job. I always put Him to the side. That is not love at all. I guess I am the backslider that He is married to. I am always leaving Him. "Jesus I do not want to keep walking away from you. I want to love you, but I do not know how to love you. Teach me to love you the way you want to be loved. I want to be a good wife to you. Teach me how. Father I want to worship, honor, and praise you in truth from the depth of my heart. Teach me how." All of a sudden "The Prayer of Deondra" became alive to me. My Father began to explain it to me.

• I must be about my Father's business, Lord teach me how, this life is meant for us to come and do the will of our Father. We get so trapped into the cares of this world that we forget the true purpose of our life. It does not matter if we have a million dollar home and car. Nothing that we have can be taken with us when we die. All is left here on earth for others to use and perhaps fight over. Why get caught up in things that can not go with you when you die? Focus on heavenly things. Deny yourself and follow Jesus. Be about God's business and He will take care of yours. Lord, teach us how to be about your business. Teach us to get our priorities straight.

• Teach me to be real in what I do and say, Our Father wants us to be real. There are enough false teachers walking around professing the name of Christ. We must learn to practice what we preach. We must live the Word as Christ did. We must do everything with love and purity in our hearts. The words of our mouth and the meditation of our hearts must be acceptable in God's sight.

• Teach me how to wait and how to pray. It is so hard waiting on an answer from God when you do not have patience. Often times we get ourselves into a lot of trouble because we rush into things from lack of patience, and we wonder why there is confusion and chaos. Prayer is your time to confess your faults, intercede, make a request known, meditate, and surrender to your heavenly Father.

• Teach me to stay humble in the work you have for me to do, before honor is humility. The highest that you will ever get above Jesus Christ is at His feet, so never try to be above Christ. Never try to take credit for anything because you are nothing without Jesus.

• Keep me in perfect peace with my mind stayed on you, there is nothing like the peace of God. This is the kind of peace where confusion and chaos can be all around you and you do not know it. If we stay focused on the Word of God and keep our mind stayed on Him, we will be kept in perfect peace. Why worry when we have someone to carry all of our cares?

• Teach me how to keep my mouth shut and my eyes open because you said to watch and pray, Christians are bad when it comes to gossiping and putting each other down. It is time to keep our mouth shut and off of other people and for once talk about ourselves to God. Tell God how filthy we are and how bad we need Him. When we tend to our own business and confess our faults to God He will cleanse us. When we see a fault in our brother or sister in Christ we should pray instead of talk about them.

• Lord keep me on my knees everyday, we need to stay before the Lord everyday. We have to be prayed up in order to have strength to fight off the enemy and temptation.

• Lord in my heart, mind, and body is where I want to keep you, if God is in our heart, mind, and body constantly imagine how pure we would be. Sink about the power we would have through Christ Jesus.

• Fill me with your love, joy, and peace when a storm comes through. Instead of worrying when trouble comes, I would rather be happy and full of peace because I know who is in control (my Father). This is when you know and trust God to take care of the situation.

• Lord there are people in this world that don't even know me but those people are depending on you to use me to bring them to thee, there are people that we as Christians have never met, but in our calling and destiny will meet in the future directly or indirectly. Those people are depending on God through prayers to send people in their paths like you and I to minister to them or give them a word of encouragement. We as Christians have to get focused and get aligned with God because we are holding up people's deliverance.

• Teach me to diligently seek you so that I can be prepared for tests, because Satan is getting wise, but God you are wisest, we must seek God's face daily. We must ask for God's decision on all that we do. Temptation is always coming to you but you have to be strong in the Lord to resist temptation. We are tested through trials, tribulation, and our weaknesses. If we study to show ourselves approved the enemy will know who we are. We just have to say "it is written". We defeat the enemy with the Word of God.

• Come into my heart and search it completely, I want everything that is not of you out of me, shine the light of heaven on my heart. Whatever is in me that is not of Christ I want it out. I want to be pure in the eyes of my Father.

• Lord I need you in my life I can't make it without you, I can't even wake up in the morning if you don't tell me to, Jesus is the source of our life. We can not live without Jesus. God can think and we would be no more. So we need Him.

• Lord I want you to know I love and honor you for just being you, I want to thank you for my life, health, and strength too, take time out just to give God thanks for being so wonderful, amazing, magnificent, powerful, and mighty. Thank Him for the little things and the things we often take for granted. Let him know you appreciate Him.

• Order my steps and keep me in your will, let Jesus be the light of your path. We need to walk in the will of God because if we rebel against His will too long He will move us out of His way.

• When you are fighting my battles help me to be still, we are not strong enough to fight battles. We have no power without Jesus. When our Father is fighting our battles we need to move out of the way and let Him do what He does best, and that is conquer.

• Let my light shine so that the world can see that I got Jesus inside of me after I am taught all I need to know and all unrighteousness is removed from me, Lord let the world see you when they look at me.

"Deondra, do you love me?"

Jesus asked me one last time do I love Him. I can finally say yes and know in my heart that I truly love Jesus Christ. I heard Him then say "feed my sheep. Go forth and spread my Word to everyone. Let them know who I am and that I love them." I said with great honor, "yes Lord".

THE ULTIMATE
FIREFIGHTER

Do you know how valuable you are to God? John 3:16 says, "For God so loved the world, that he gave his only begotten Son, that whosoever believeth in him should not perish but have everlasting life." You are a prized possession in God's eyes. You were fearfully and wonderfully made. This world was in a mess, and God needed somebody who He could trust and who He knew would be faithful to clean up the mess of the world. He needed a ransom. The only one worthy of the ransom was His Son Jesus. So He sent His only Son into this world to save you and I.

Imagine for a moment waking up in the morning and you smell smoke. What is the first thing that will run across your mind? "I smell smoke, so there must be a fire." Now imagine that this smoke is very thick. You drop out of your bed and you get on the floor and crawl through the house until you can get to safety. It may even get to the point to where you have to crawl on your belly to safety. Once you make it outside, you here somebody scream "help". That person who screamed is your child. Now you look at your house and fire is almost covering the whole house. What is your next move? Do you go and try to save your child, or do you wait on the firefighter? Well, each parent may have their own opinion on what they would do. Aren't you glad to have that parent that would not hesitate to save you, even if it cost them their life?

Living for Christ is the best way to live this life. We as Christians are going to go through some trying times throughout this journey. The thing to remember is to keep running the race. Don't quit. Help is on the way. Let's take a look at this fire in a spiritual sense. Your home represents your life. The smoke is symbolic of trouble or sin. We as Christians can not afford to sleep on the job. The Bible says that we must watch and pray. Sleeping on the job can cause us our lives. Some people die in fires because they were asleep and they woke up too late. When trouble comes in our lives it is up to us to see our way out. Smoke, in the natural, can cause you to suffocate. Smoke takes up all of the space of oxygen. Most people die in fires because of the intoxication of the smoke, and not necessarily the fire. The wages of sin is death. When we recognize that we have trouble or sin (smoke) in our homes (lives) we try to find a way out of the house. We can not stand up tall and walk out of a house full of smoke. We have to crawl (humble) our way out of the house. Crawling represents praying.

One thing that I realized in this journey is that God requires you to give him some of your time. If you do not give him time willingly, he will bring things in your life to cause you to give him time, hence smoke. Trying times will bring you to your knees. This is a season where we as Christians need to pray and seek God's face. Trouble is in the land and a lot of Christians are sleeping on the job. Wake up. Don't die in the fire. God said He will take you through the fire and bring you out. Trust and believe. I know that the smoke is thick. Lay on your belly and crawl your way out. It is time to lay prostrate before the Lord to hear his voice. There may be an instance where you are in the burning house and you are on your belly but the fire is too great for you. Your instincts tell you to do the only thing you know and that is yell for help, even if you do not think anyone is around to hear you, you still yell help in hope. You hope that someone will hear you in the fire. Guess who our hope is when we are in a great fire? Jesus Christ. When you are in trouble and you yell from your belly "Jesus save me", He will come to your rescue. It does not matter to him how severe the fire is. He already gave his life for us, so He has nothing to lose. Jesus himself had to go through a fire. He had to lose his life to safe ours. He is that parent that will go and save his child from the fire if that child cries for help. Jesus is the ultimate firefighter. Always remember in times of trouble to STOP, DROP, and PRAY. The ultimate firefighter will come to your rescue.

I am at a point right now where I am so in love with Jesus. I feel as light as a feather. He makes me feel so safe and secure. Now that I have developed a closer relationship with Jesus, I am able to make a greater connection with my Father. I realize now that Jesus really loves me. I have never experienced this kind of love ever before in my life. Jesus said all I have to do is ask in His name and He will do it. I can come and talk to Him when I have a problem, or when I feel heavy, and just give it all to Him and let Him carry the heaviness. That is amazing. Jesus is the best high that I have ever had. I wish that I would have never left Jesus because this is the greatest and most peaceful feeling in the world.

ABOUT THE AUTHOR

I was born and raised in Cordele, Georgia. I gave my life to Christ at age 19. I have always known that I would be an author. I have been writing book since I was a kid but never had the guts to publish them. I decided in 2009 that I would hearken to the voice of my father and minister to the world through my books.